MARVEL
AVENGERS
INFINITY WAR

"It's all been leading to this!"

From the bustling streets of New York City to the majestic world of Asgard... From the mysterious, hidden kingdom of Wakanda to the alien worlds comprising of the Nova Empire... The Marvel Cinematic Universe has taken audiences on an incredible journey where imagination and adventure know no bounds.

We have followed the stories of the founding members of the Avengers: Tony Stark, Steve Rogers, Natasha Romanoff, Clint Barton, and Bruce Banner and the recruits who joined their cause as they led by example.

But now, as Thanos executes his scheme to collect the 6 Infinity Stones and wreak havoc upon the universe, heroes will unite in an attempt to stop him, no matter what the cost....

THE OFFICIAL MARVEL MOVIE SPECIALS
Thor: Ragnarok
Black Panther
Avengers: Infinity War
Ant-Man and the Wasp (July 2018)

TITAN EDITORIAL

Editor Jonathan Wilkins
Senior Editor Martin Eden
Editorial Assistants Tolly Maggs
& Jake Devine
Art Director Oz Browne
Senior Production Controller Jackie Flook
Production Supervisor Maria Pearson
Production Controller Peter James
Senior Sales Manager Santosh Maharaj
Subscriptions Executive Tony Ho

Direct Sales & Marketing Manager
Ricky Claydon
Advertising Assistant Bella Hoy
Commercial Manager Michelle Fairlamb
Circulation Assistant Frankie Hallam
Brand Manager, Marketing Lucy Ripper
U.S. Advertising Manager Jeni Smith
Publishing Manager Darryl Tothill
Publishing Director Chris Teather
Operations Director Leigh Baulch
Executive Director Vivian Cheung
Publisher Nick Landau

DISTRIBUTION
US Newsstand: Total Publisher Services, Inc.
John Dziewiatkowski, 630-851-7683
US Distribution: Curtis Circulation Company,
Ingram Periodicals
US Direct Sales Market: Diamond
Comic Distributors
For more info on advertising contact
adinfo@titanemail.com

Marvel Studios' *Avengers: Infinity War* published May 2018
by Titan Magazines, a division of Titan Publishing Group
Limited, 144 Southwark Street, London SE1 0UP.
For sale in the U.S. and Canada.

ISBN: 9781785868054

Printed in the US by Quad
Contributors Nick Jones, Darren Scott
Thank you to Shiho Tilley, Beatrice Osman, and
Eugene Paraszczuk at Disney for all their help.

Titan Authorized User. No part of this publication may be
reproduced, stored in a retrival system, or transmitted,
in any form or by any means, without the prior written
permission of the publisher. A CIP catalogue record for
this title is available from the British Library.

10 9 8 7 6 5 4 3 2 1

marvel.com
© 2018 MARVEL

DISNEY PUBLISHING WORLDWIDE Global Magazines, Comics and Partworks
Publisher: Lynn Waggoner. Editorial Director: Bianca Coletti.
Editorial Team: Guido Frazzini (Director, Comics), Stefano Ambrosio (Executive Editor, New IP), Carlotta Quattrocolo (Executive Editor, Franchise), Camilla Vedove (Senior Manager,
Editorial Development), Behnoosh Khalili (Senior Editor), Julie Dorris (Senior Editor). Design: Enrico Soave (Senior Designer). Art: Ken Shue (VP, Global Art),
Roberto Santillo (Creative Director), Marco Ghiglione (Creative Manager), Manny Mederos (Creative Manager), Stefano Attardi (Illustration Manager)
Portfolio Management: Olivia Ciancarelli (Director) Business & Marketing: Mariantonietta Galla (Senior Manager, Franchise), Virpi Korhonen (Editorial Manager).

CONTENTS

CREATING THE WAR

Visit the *Avengers: Infinity War* set as the President of Marvel Studios and producer, Kevin Feige, writers Chris Markus and Stephen McFeely, directors the Russo Brothers and, Mr. Marvel himself, Stan Lee discuss the making of the film.

01

KEVIN FEIGE

How did you bring all of these characters together for *Infinity War*?

Kevin Feige: This feels like the culmination of something that's been building for years and years, and really the closest thing is the experience we had on the first *Avengers* film when Chris Hemsworth as Thor, Chris Evans as Captain America, and Robert Downey Jr. as Tony Stark met together in the woods for the first time. Even seeing the three of them in a piece of concept art together for the first time gave us a thrill. At that point the other films hadn't come out. All we knew was that audiences loved Robert Downey Jr. as Tony Stark. They had never seen Cap or Thor yet. What's happening now feels like that times a thousand.

Many of the characters that are appearing in this film have never appeared together before but have already had numerous films that the audiences have responded to. You can feel the excitement even with the crew when Chris Pratt walks out and does his first scene with Tom Holland and Robert Downey Jr., or when Chris Hemsworth as Thor encounters the Guardians for the first time. There is just something chemically awesome about seeing these different franchise heroes interacting with each other for the first time. And when you think about it, we haven't really seen that since the first *Avengers* film. *Avengers: Age of Ultron* introduced some new characters within the body of that film, and *Captain America: Civil War* introduced Black Panther and Spider-Man within the body of that film, which was great. But the notion of seeing characters who you've grown to love in their own movies walking into another movie for the first time at a deep human evolutionary level is satisfying.

You've been able to fill this universe with great actors...

The amount of actors in this film is staggering. Seeing the amount of A-list actors who carry their own movies elsewhere all joining us on this one is one of the great joys of making this movie.

Josh Brolin is amazing. It's so satisfying to hear him say these lines and to interact with these other characters. We've been teasing this for six years. That's a long time to tease something cinematically before paying it off. He has to be the greatest villain in the history of the Marvel Cinematic Universe.

It looks like the cast and crew are really having fun!

It is the biggest film we've ever made. It is the longest production period that we've ever had. Every day is fun because I think everyone – from the A-list cast to the people who are putting together the wonderful food for the crew to eat – know that we're doing something special for the ages.

Can you enjoy the film if you aren't up to speed on the Marvel Studios movies to date?

We believe that every movie we make needs to feel like a standalone piece of entertainment – that you can walk ▶

▶ in cold and enjoy, with a beginning, middle and end. We always ask that question in our research screenings. Do you feel you needed to have seen the other movies?

People who have not seen the other movies say 'No.' People who have seen the other movies can see the connections. That's the balance that we want to find: making a film that will appeal to people who've never seen one of our movies. It's an entertaining self-contained story, but it will work on a much deeper level for people who are following along. There are a lot of pay-offs in this film that go back to the first *Iron Man* movie.

The audience is emotionally connected with these characters. Are these heroes going to be challenged in a way that's going to be emotionally devastating?
Of all the films we've made, *Infinity War* will have the greatest repercussions by far, and things will not be the same when the credits start to roll (for the Marvel Cinematic Universe). We've had fun in all the movies. There will be fun in *Infinity War*. But there's high stakes and loss in *Infinity War* that will not be easily undone. Again we tap into experiences that we had as fans reading the comics and that we've had as fans watching our favorite movies, and there comes a point where there needs to be finality and storytelling.

What's great about the entire team, is the way they handle humor and drama. There will be tragedy in *Infinity War*, there will be drama in *Infinity War*, but there is also inherent humor as Doctor Strange meets Tony Stark for the first time, and as the Guardians of the Galaxy encounter Thor. Some of our characters who have previously been earthbound find themselves having a conversation with a tree and a raccoon! At the same time, Thanos means business, and he's not messing around. The characters will be tested in much deeper and darker ways than they ever have been. There will be great humor with the Guardians meeting the Avengers, but at the same time there will probably be shocking drama, and it's certainly much darker than we've ever had before.

Has there been a moment over the last ten years where you realized what you were setting up was going to be a success?

01 (Previous spread) A key scene involving Chris Hemsworth and Josh Brolin (in motion capture suit) is filmed

02 An impressive set dominates the studio space

03 Karen Gillan and Zoe Saldana shoot a complicated visual effects scene

04 A cheerful Josh Brolin on set

05 Thor finds himself in unfamilar surroundings

> ## "*Infinity War* will have the greatest repercussions by far. Things will not be the same when the credits roll."

I think the success of *Iron Man* was amazing for a new studio launching its first film. That gave us the confidence to do another *Iron Man* film, and a *Captain America* film, and to introduce Thor the God of Thunder from Asgard. It was the success of the first *Avengers* film that taught us that the audience really gets what we're doing and really enjoys the cross pollination of all of these different film series. That allowed us to plot out everything that we've done since then, and everything specifically building to *Infinity War*.

CHRIS MARKUS AND STEPHEN MCFEELY

How exciting and funny is it getting these characters together?
Chris Markus: They mesh very well together. There's something about Peter Quill's idiocy and Tony's arrogance! They irritate each other for hours.
Stephen McFeely: It was really nice to see a frustrated Tony Stark as kind of the straight man, because usually he's the one that gets to cause chaos. And now he is the one that's trying to organize people.
CM: Basically there's like a bubble coming out of his head saying, "Now I know how Steve feels!"

Robert Downey Jr. and Tom Holland already have chemistry…
SM: Robert and Tom have had two movies already but it was bubbling away even in Tom's auditions with Robert.

CM: Doctor Strange is yet another person who's in opposition to Tony and Peter ends up taking sides between them. It's delightful.

How do you start writing a movie like this?
SM: We're big structure guys, so we lay out the story with all the possible people that could be in the movie and then sort of whittle it down to who have arcs to tell and stories to tell. And then how can we group them in such a way that they get enough time to explore those arcs but without dominating the entire movie? So when you see the movie you'll see that it's sort of woven into four or five parts. We'll be cutting back and forth between those parts.
CM: No one is stronger than Thanos. He can punch everybody in the face better than they can punch him back in the face. But he's got daughters and goals, a past and an ego that can be dented, and that's where you have to begin weaving him in order to make him a believable villain. Occasionally I think he's the good guy.
SM: Our philosophy is we may not agree with our villains, but we believe *they* believe what they're doing and they believe *in* what they're doing. That goes for [undercover Hydra operative] Alexander Pierce or [terrorist] Helmut Zemo. I don't think they're doing the right thing, but I know they *think* they're doing the right thing. And the same goes with Thanos. He's just kind of bigger and more purple!

THE RUSSO BROTHERS

How closely do you follow the original Marvel comics?
Joe Russo: Anything we do with the comics is an inspiration; it's a jumping off point. We have storytelling that's more specific to the Marvel Cinematic Universe. It's been such a long journey for these Marvel films. For me - not only as a director who's been on a journey with these movies, but as a comic book fan, seeing these characters together, knowing what it means for these movies and that all of this carefully crafted storytelling is now coming to a head in this film - that is just staggering.

06

It must feel extra special to see these characters at this stage of their development.
JR: It's been very earned, very meticulously crafted. It's the same creative group that worked on *Winter Soldier* and *Civil War*. It's Anthony and I and Markus and McFeely. Together the four of us crafted a plan moving forward for all of these characters, how we want to see them used, through our sense of storytelling.

Avengers: Infinity War has an epic nature. How does it sit with the other movies?
JR: I think if the first ten years of Marvel films were a book, this is the final parts of the story, and this movie would be the final chapter. So the fourth *Avengers* film brings everything to a head and closes everything in the first three phases of the Marvel Cinematic Universe and starts a new beginning for Phase 4.

What's it like seeing these characters come to a close?
Anthony Russo: These are characters that the actors have lived with for many years, so it's intense for them. It represents a lot of work in their life, in a chapter of their lives. Everybody is really putting their most into what these scenes can be, the whole crew, the producers, figuring out what is the most elegant, exciting, surprising, and satisfying version of how their stories end.

Are you looking forward to the combination of 20 to 30 actors in one scene?
AR: Yes. These movies are certainly the most complex

06 Thanos' heavies prepare to shoot a key scene

07 Tom Holland dons a motion capture suit as he checks out his performance on the monitors

08 *The Milano* in the studio. Don't worry, the effects will be added in later!

> "These movies are among the most complex things that have ever been attempted in filmmaking. But we're up for the challenge."
> - Anthony Russo

things we've ever attempted as filmmakers, and they're among the most complex things that have ever been attempted in filmmaking. But we have the most amazing team working with us and we're up for the challenge.

What has it been like working with Markus and McFeely?
JR: The great thing about having collaborators, and the four of us having worked together for so many years, is that there is never an opportunity to settle, because somebody's always pushing the group forward. We have a very rigorous process by which the screenplays are executed. It involves a lot of time in a room together talking through character, motive, story structure, themes, and plot twists. It's a very intense period. It can take us

THE
SPACE
STONE

Contained within a cube-like structure known as the Tesseract, the Space Stone grants the user instant unimpeded access to anywhere in the universe.

01

TIMELESS DANGER

The Space Stone first appeared in *Captain America: The First Avenger*. Contained in the form of a cube-like structure known as the Tesseract of Odin, Johann Schmidt a.k.a. the Red Skull, stole it from its hiding place in an ancient church in Tønsberg in Norway.

The Red Skull was Nazi Germany's first Super-Soldier. The Super-Soldier Serum that gave Steve Rogers his power as Captain America had been developed by Abraham Erskine, and Johann Schmidt injected himself with it before it had been perfected. It gave him strength, speed, and agility but it also had a terrible effect upon his skin, giving him a red, cadaverous face, which he would hide behind a mask of his former visage.

As head of Hydra (the scientific research branch of the Nazis in WWII, which would go on to become an organization bent on world domination), the Red Skull decided to use the Tesseract to power an advanced super bomber that he planned to use against the United States.

The Red Skull was to find out the hard way what happens to lesser mortals when they attempt to touch one of these stones without the benefit of protective covering. Upon touching the stone, he was transported into a portal across space, never to be seen again. After the Skull's defeat, the Tesseract was recovered from the bottom of the ocean and was to remain in S.H.I.E.L.D. custody until 2012. S.H.I.E.L.D., the Strategic Homeland Intervention, Enforcement and Logistics Division, a US extra-governmental military counter-terrorism and intelligence agency, was formed after WWII to protect the United States — and then later the world — from any kind of threat.

MISCHIEF IN THE AIR

After 70 years of inactivity, the Tesseract became the subject of a terrible deal between Loki, brother to Thor, and Thanos, the mad Titan. Loki agreed to retrieve the Tesseract for Thanos, in exchange for the use of Thanos's army of Chitauri, who would help him conquer Earth.

Thanos, a ruthless cosmic warlord, does not suffer disappointment lightly, and Loki was warned that if he failed to retrieve the Tesseract for Thanos, he would pay a terrible price.

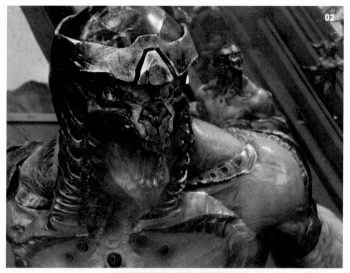

INVASION

Not long after stealing the Tesseract, Loki succeeded in using it to open a portal in space, and soon the Chitauri invaders were pouring through. Things looked bleak for the world, but the Avengers assembled for the first time and managed to beat them back and get control of the Tesseract. Loki suffered a severe beating at the hands of the Hulk, which he would never forget, and was then taken to Asgard by Thor.

Considered too dangerous to remain on Earth, Thor took the Tesseract with him back to Asgard and placed it in the safe keeping of his friend and fellow Asgardian, Heimdall. ⒶA

PREVIOUS WIELDERS OF THE SPACE STONE

Cosmic Entities
Odin
Church Keeper
The Red Skull
Howard Stark
S.H.I.E.L.D.
Loki
Heimdall

POSTSCRIPT

During the events of *Thor: Ragnarok*, it was implied that Loki had managed to get his hands on the Tesseract once again. He may wield the stone, but with Thanos getting closer by the day, will he be able to enjoy it for long?

THE
MIND
STONE

The Mind Stone grants the user the ability to control the minds of other sentient beings. However, that barely scratches the surface of its capabilities – for this Infinity Stone can also be used as a weapon and as a creative force, the likes of which Earth has never seen before...

MIND OVER MATTER

The Mind Stone was first introduced into the Marvel Cinematic Universe in *The Avengers* back in 2012. Thanos, unaware of what it actually was, granted use of the stone to Loki to help him in his proposed conquest of Earth.

When it first appeared it was contained in the form of a scepter, and it allowed Loki to fire energy blasts from its tip and also granted him the ability to communicate mentally with the being known as the Other, the servant of Thanos.

Loki's scepter also managed to subtly affect the minds of the Avengers, making them bicker and turn against each other. When the tip of the scepter is placed against a victim's heart, a blue energy is transferred into their body, turning their eyes a translucent blue color as they fall completely under the mental control of the stone. Loki did this to Hawkeye, and it was only after receiving a blow to the head that the bow-slinging Avenger was able to reassert control of his own mind and free himself from Loki's influence.

CONNECTIONS

Following Loki's defeat at the hands of his brother, Thor, Black Widow placed the scepter into the care of S.H.I.E.L.D. Nicholas Cooper, one of the researchers tasked with studying the scepter was the first to draw

a connection between it and the Tesseract; however, his studies were cut short when the scepter was stolen by agents of Hydra. The artifact was then taken to a Hydra research facility in Sokovia, where Wolfgang von Strucker, a leader of the group, soon ordered that it be used in experiments on humans. Large numbers of volunteers were taken from among the Sokovian populace, but all of them died during the experiments, except for the twins Wanda and Pietro Maximoff, who gained extraordinary powers as a result.

ULTRON

The Avengers recaptured the scepter after raiding the research facility in *Avengers: Age of Ultron*. Thor wanted to take the scepter to Asgard for safekeeping, but Tony Stark asked his friend for permission to study it first. Stark believed that the stone contained an artificial intelligence that could make his dream of a global peacekeeping initiative — known as Ultron — become a reality. Ultron, however, believed that mankind was the greatest threat to world peace, and set about his mission to destroy humanity. He stole the scepter and allied himself with Pietro and Wanda Maximoff. They were to turn against him when they learned of his genocidal intentions.

He used the power of the Mind Stone to force geneticist Helen Cho to help him build a perfect body

01 Loki wields the Mind Stone within his scepter

02 Hawkeye under the spell of the Mind Stone

03 An army of Ultron sentries seek to wipe out humanity

04 Wanda and Pietro Maximoff were given superhuman powers by the Mind Stone

05 Ultron used the Mind Stone to create Vision

06 Ultron the homicidal AI

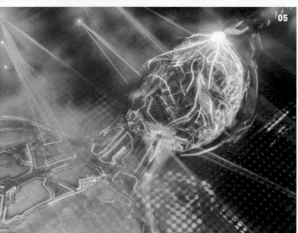

encased in the rare metal vibranium. He then broke the Mind Stone out of the scepter in order to power the perfect body.

VISION

The Mind Stone was embedded into the forehead of this body, which allied itself with the Avengers against Ultron. This new AI was to become known as Vision and was to prove an invaluable ally in the battle to come against Ultron's army of Ultron Sentries. The stone in his forehead allows him to fire energy blasts and to alter his density, becoming incredibly heavy or to become wraithlike and phase through walls at will. The stone remains a mystery to Vision but he hopes to one day understand it so that, instead of controlling him, he will be able to exert control over it.

REMOTE CONTROL

During *Captain America: Civil War*, Vision was guarding Wanda Maximoff at the New Avengers Facility. Captain America wanted to free Wanda, and he sent Hawkeye to break her out of the facility. When Vision tried to stop the archer, Wanda used her powers to exert control over the Mind Stone and forced him to release them before slamming him down deep into the ground, giving her time to escape and join Captain America. Ⓐ

PREVIOUS WIELDERS OF THE MIND STONE

Cosmic Entities
Thanos
Loki
S.H.I.E.L.D.
Hydra
Avengers
Ultron
Vision

REALIZATION

During the events of *Avengers: Age of Ultron*, Thor had a vision which revealed that the scepter did in fact contain the Mind Stone, one of six Inifinity Stones. It was his intention to take the stone back to Asgard, but after Vision proved himself worthy, when he was able to lift Thor's hammer, he decided to allow the stone to remain with the android, who would act as its appointed guardian. Will Vision be able to retain it when Thanos comes searching for it?

THE REALITY STONE

Introduced into the Marvel Cinematic Universe in *Thor: The Dark World*, the Reality Stone, or the Aether, as it is otherwise known, is a force of catastrophic power, capable of transforming the entire universe as it converts matter into dark matter.

LET THERE BE DARKNESS

The Reality Stone is unique, even by the standards of the Infinity Stones, in that it is not really a stone, but is in fact, a red, viscous liquid. There are, however, several theories that state that at one time, long ago, it was actually a stone, just like the others.

The first recorded use of the Reality Stone was as a weapon of the Dark Elves, thousands of years ago. It was wielded in the form of the Aether by Malekith, ruler of the Dark Elves, who wanted to transform the universe back into a place of eternal night.

The Asgardians under the rule of Bor, grandfather to Odin, realizing that Malekith's plan to plunge the universe into perpetual darkness would bring death to countless life-forms, set out to thwart Malekith's plans. After a fierce battle with heavy losses on both sides, the Dark Elves retreated in disarray and it was believed that Malekith had perished. Sadly, he was merely hibernating.

INFESTATION

Bor had the Aether hidden away and nothing more was heard of it, until 2013 when astrophysicist Jane Foster, the girlfriend of Thor, entered a portal between dimensions and found herself in the same location as the Aether. When she let curiosity get the better of her and made contact with it, the Infinity Stone became active and infested her body, using it as a host.

Upon her return to Earth she displayed unusual energy projections when touched, and Thor took her to Asgard, where his father, Odin, recognized it as the work of the Aether. Malekith also sensed its presence and awoke from hibernation eager to attack Asgard. He almost captured Jane, but Thor's mother, Frigga, sacrificed herself to stop him, and his forces fled empty-handed.

THE CONVERGENCE

Contact with the Aether was making Jane ill, and unless it could be removed from her body she would soon die. Thor, Jane and Loki traveled to Svartalfheim, the realm of the Dark Elves, where they confronted Malekith. He drew the Aether out of Jane and into himself before heading to Earth to bring endless night to the universe.

This was the time of a cosmic event known as the Convergence, which happens once every five thousand years. During the Convergence, the realms of reality become aligned and the boundaries between each dimension become exceedingly thin. These were perfect conditions for Malekith to attempt to alter reality and bring about his longed-for age of darkness. Thor battled him as he unleashed the power of the Aether, and Malekith was killed during the battle.

01 Jane Foster was infested with the Aether

02 Odin, ruler of Asgard

03 The Aether is unleashed into the atmosphere

04 The Dark Elves seek eternal night

05 Malekith, the cruel leader of the Dark Elves

04

SAFE HANDS

Because Asgard was already home to the Tesseract, the Asgardians believed the Aether should be kept safe in another location, and they entrusted it to Taneleer Tivan, otherwise known as the Collector. They did not realize that he secretly had plans to collect all of the Infinity Stones for himself and was already close to getting his hands on the Power Stone. Ⓐ

PREVIOUS WIELDERS
OF THE REALITY STONE

Cosmic Entities
Malekith
Bor
Jane Foster
Malekith
Asgard
The Collector

DEADLY POWER

The Aether seeks out a host body and will draw strength from its life force, eventually killing the host. Lesser beings will sicken and die if exposed to it for long. But Malekith was a strong host, so it enhanced his strength, giving him the power to fight Thor on an equal basis. Dark Elves such as Malekith have a special connection to the Aether, which allowed him to survive much longer than most lesser beings.

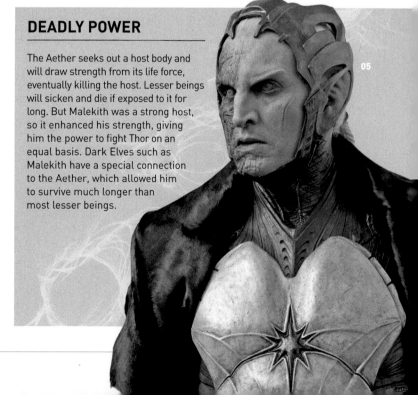

05

THE POWER STONE

Introduced in 2014's *Guardians of the Galaxy*, the Power Stone represents the destructive nature of the universe and is capable of annihilating entire planets. It is little wonder then that some of the most dangerous beings in the galaxy have hunted for it.

HARNESSING UNLIMITED POWER

Eson the Searcher, a ruthless Celestial, used the Power Stone to destroy an entire planet. His reasons for doing this have never been known, yet it stands as a reminder that power does most certainly corrupt. Since those early days, the Power Stone has also been used by a group of nine Cosmic Beings, who hoped that by linking themselves together they would be able to harness its energy. Tragically, they were mistaken – and the resulting burst of power completely overwhelmed them and led to their almost instantaneous deaths.

After the Cosmic Beings' disastrous attempt to use it ended in failure, the Power Stone was safely contained in a protective orb and sealed within a tomb on the oceanic planet of Morag. This tomb was submerged deep beneath Morag's watery surface for eons but, over the years, the ocean receded, laying bare the temple vault's secret treasure — and eventually, this treasure was sought out and discovered by none other than the cosmic adventurer, Peter Quill, a.k.a. Star-Lord.

Star-Lord was blissfully unaware that Thanos had also become aware of the Power Stone's location and had charged its retrieval to the Kree warlord, Ronan the Accuser. Ronan sent his minion, Korath the Pursuer, to Morag, but he failed to prevent Star-Lord from escaping with the treasure. Needless to say, this did not go down well with the galaxy's most nefarious overlord.

01 Ronan the Accuser

02 Star-Lord comes face-to-face with the Orb

03 The Cosmic Beings attempt to use the Power Stone

04 The battle for Xandar

05 The Guardians of the Galaxy harness the energy of the Power Stone

06

THE POWER UNLEASHED

The danger of the Power Stone was revealed when Star-Lord tried to sell it to Taneleer Tivan, a.k.a. the Collector. With the Orb's casing open, his assistant dared to touch the stone itself, causing an explosion that nearly destroyed them all. Ronan pounced to take the Orb for himself, defying Thanos and placing the Power Stone on his Cosmi-Rod, giving him incredible power.

Ronan then decided to attack the planet Xandar. His own species, the Kree, had a long history of enmity toward the Xandarians, and Ronan had been furious when the two empires had signed a peace treaty. He decided to use the Power Stone to destroy his enemies and the Nova Corps who protected the planet.

He was confronted by the Guardians of the Galaxy, and although he was more powerful than any of them, he became distracted by Star-Lord's dancing, which gave Drax the opportunity to destroy his Cosmi-Rod. As the Power Stone became dislodged, Star-Lord grasped it before Ronan could react.

IN THE HANDS OF FATE

Star-Lord was able to survive the Stone's energy thanks to his team of Guardians, who joined hands with him to distribute the power of the Stone. Quill's half-celestial lineage also played a part in his survival as the Stone's energy was directed at Ronan, killing him instantly.

After the battle, the Power Stone was handed over to the Nova Corps for safekeeping in their headquarters on Xandar. ⊕

PREVIOUS WIELDERS OF THE POWER STONE

Cosmic Entities
Eson the Searcher
Cosmic Beings
Peter Quill (Star-Lord)
Ronan the Accuser
Nova Corps

06 Ronan and Star-Lord race to grab the Power Stone

07 Rhomann Dey of the Nova Corps

07

THE NOVA CORPS

The military and police force of the Nova Empire, the Nova Corps have been on the front lines of a 1,000-year war with the Kree Empire, until peace finally came in 2014. Based on Xandar, they are led by Nova Prime and they are now firm allies of the Guardians of the Galaxy. They make formidable foes and are an excellent choice for guarding one of the most dangerous devices in the known universe.

THE
TIME
STONE

Granting its wielder the ability to control the flow of time
on a small or an epic scale, the Time Stone has the power
to alter both the past and the future...

THE EYE OF AGAMOTTO

Created by Agamotto, the first Sorceror Supreme, the Eye acts as a container for the Time Stone, allowing the user to unleash its power without suffering any terrible consequences. Created in the shape of an eye, the relic can be used only by someone adept at the mystic arts. The Eye itself must be opened before the stone can be used, and to do this, the user must first know the correct spells and gestures required to make it work.

The Eye of Agamotto was housed in Kamar-Taj in Kathmandu, Nepal, the home of The Ancient One and training center for the Masters of the Mystic Arts. It was here that it was found by Doctor Stephen Strange while on a journey of self discovery.

ALTERNATE TIMELINES

Doctor Strange first tested the Eye's power on an apple, reversing and forwarding time on the fruit. He then used it on the Book of Cagliostro, a mystic book that revealed the presence of the Dark Dimension and its powerful overlord, Dormammu. But Doctor Strange stopped using the Eye when Wong and Karl Mordo warned him that he was creating different alternate timelines, something which could potentially destroy the natural order of things. However, Strange was to use the relic once more before too long, as his order, and Earth itself came under attack from Kaecilius, a former student of The Ancient One, who now sought to bring the Dread Dormammu, Lord of the Dark Dimension, to Earth in exchange for real power.

01 The ancient Book of Cagliostro, which reveals the secrets of the Eye of Agamotto

02 Lost in another dimension

03 Doctor Strange utilizes the Eye of Agamotto

TURN BACK TIME

Doctor Strange used the Eye of Agamotto to turn back time after the Hong Kong Sanctum of the Masters of the Mystic Arts was destroyed by Kaecilius and his Zealots. He brought his friend Wong back to life, along with others who had died in the attack, but before he could restore the Sanctum, he was stopped by Kaecilius. Kaecilius told Strange that he could not stop Dormammu entering our world and that the gateway to the Dark Dimension would soon be open.

Strange used the Eye to freeze time and then headed straight into the Dark Dimension, creating a time loop while he tried to negotiate with Dormammu, who simply ignored his offer of peace and destroyed him with ease.

Before Dormammu could return his thoughts to the conquest of Earth, Strange reappeared and repeated his offer. Dormammu was confused and demanded to know what was happening. Strange explained that he had trapped them both in a time loop without end and that events would repeat until Dormammu agreed to listen to him.

AN ETERNITY OF PAIN

In his rage, Dormammu killed Strange again and again and again. He promised Strange an eternity of pain and anguish as he attempted to get his adversary to break the loop in time. Strange replied that it was a price worth paying, if it would protect the lives of everyone on Earth.

The Dark Dimension is a realm where time does not exist. This left Dormammu powerless to stop Strange,

or to break the loop. In the end, exhausted, Dormammu relented and asked Strange what it was that he wanted.

In exchange for breaking the time loop, Doctor Strange made Dormammu swear never to return to Earth and to take the Zealots with him. Dormammu had no option but to accept these terms and surrender. The Time Stone had saved Earth from the horrors of the Dark Dimension. Doctor Strange then returned to Hong Kong, moments before his departure. Kaecilius was surprised and then horrified, when he learned that his foe had entered into a bargain with Dormammu. He barely had time to react before Dormammu turned Kaecilius and his Zealots into Mindless Ones and took them with him to the Dark Dimension.

DANGEROUS

Having used the Time Stone to restore Hong Kong to its natural state from before the attack, Strange decided he was not ready to wear the Eye of Agamotto and he returned it to Kamar-Taj. It was then that Wong revealed to him that the Eye was in fact an Infinity Stone and that overusing such a relic was incredibly dangerous. Whether the Eye is permanently in Kamar-Taj these days is unknown, for Doctor Strange appeared to be wearing the relic when he helpin Thor and Loki locate their father, Odin. ⚡

PREVIOUS WIELDERS OF THE TIME STONE

Cosmic Entities
Agamotto
Cagliostro
Sorcerors Supreme
The Eye of Agamotto is passed down to each successive Sorceror Supreme. Therefore, the previous owner of the Eye was The Ancient One.

OPEN THE EYE

Agamotto established the Sanctums and the Eye of Agamotto, which was created to contain the energy of the Time Stone, was named after him.

04 Doctor Strange puts his mystic training into practice

05 The Eye of Agamotto

05

ROBERT DOWNEY JR.
IRON MAN

The character that kicked off the Marvel Cinematic Universe was Iron Man, played by charismatic force of nature, Robert Downey Jr. Ten years on, Downey Jr. suits up for Iron Man's toughest battle yet…

Did you see what was to come in the wake of the first *Iron Man* movie?
Yes, although not due to any particular intellectual capacity of my own, but intuitively. It's like if you go to a vintage clothing store, and see a really cool jacket that nobody's bought. Batman was already being re-launched, Spider-Man had just come in and become a sensation – there was this sense that there was a resurgence.

Stan Lee's iteration of Tony Stark was rooted in my generation; that Vietnam kind of anti-establishment but also hearkening to the kind of Howard Hughes eccentric billionaire thing was just so cool. I thought modernizing it at the time of another American conflict made it relevant again. The effects, which hitherto would have been too challenging or would have looked bad, were made possible thanks to innovations in filmmaking. It was a perfect storm.

Over the years, what's changed with Iron Man's suits?
If you're first on sight for an innovation you go through all of the models until you get to a working model. I have no complaints about any of the suits I ever wore because they worked for exactly what we needed them to. I remember once being on a rooftop, and I'm wearing all these suit pieces, and they put the helmet on me and lit up the lights. All I could see was the inside of the circuitry of the helmet. They said to take about five steps forward and it was an exercise in faith.

But even on this new movie we were shooting a scene that completely reminded me of the old Tony workshop days. And so the Tao of super hero filmmaking, at least as it's unfolded in the Marvel Cinematic Universe, has remained very much the same.

Did you find Tony's humanity on the set or on the page?
When I think about the progenitor super hero films, I think what was absent in them was a sense of bringing a new twist on the material – even though, at the time, I felt like those films met all my needs. I think that Jon [Favreau] brings a naturalism and an ease and an unscripted nature to what he does. And yet for him, as the original gangster as far as who's running the ship on these things, he looked to me and Gwyneth like, *Alright, now how do we make these characters really relatable and fun?*

But I think we can all understand metaphorically the love of a good woman and witness a transition in a kind of a broken guy. And then we had Jeff Bridges. When you bring in literally an iconic veteran as the bad guy, you've already won.

How did you find the chemistry with Gwyneth Paltrow?
I think this was the beginnings of her thinking about doing web commerce or something like that, so Gwyneth, aside from the fact that she's obviously a national treasure as an actress, has done her version of what Pepper Potts would've done if Tony Stark had passed out and died in the bathroom halfway through the first *Iron Man* movie. We had a scene in the movie where they built me a whole dummy chest and body. Jon Favreau said we can't do that practically, but I want everyone to get the feeling that she's literally digging around inside your chest cavity and we're gonna somehow or other dig out ▶

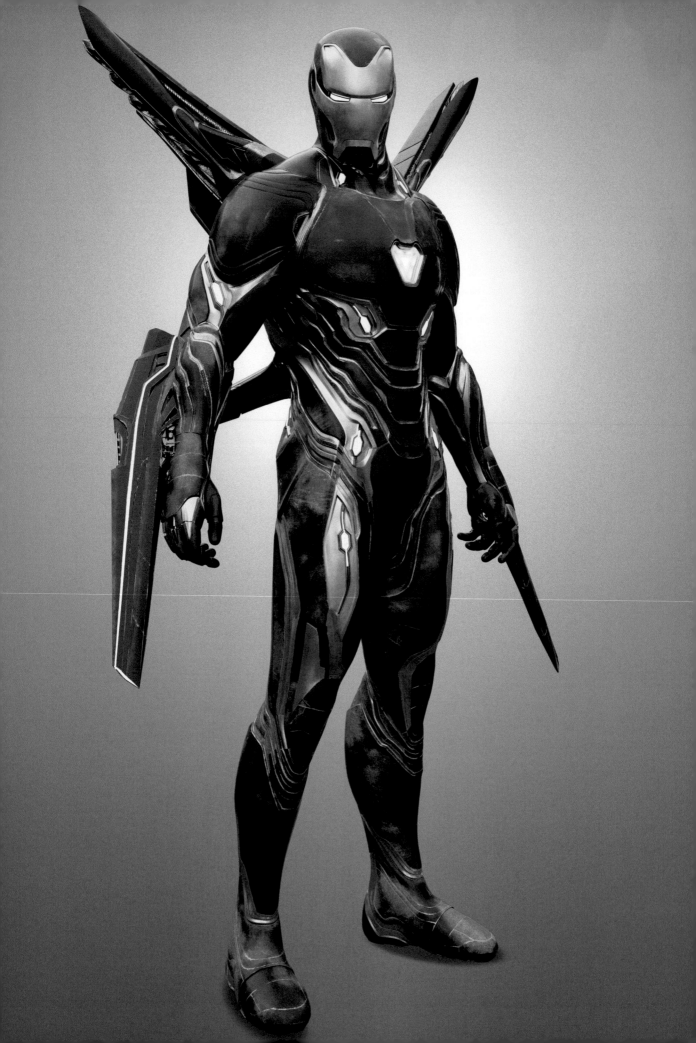

01

"Thanos is essentially the least defeatable guy. Tony knows that it's a different game now."

▶ intimacy and vulnerability and connection from that moment. It's always been a case of humanity first with these films.

Did you feel everything was working well on camera?
Yeah, when I was shooting the first *Iron Man* film, I had hypnotized myself into such a state of confidence that I was certain that everything we were doing worked. As it turned out, a little less than 70 percent worked. They cut out the 30 percent and focused on that 70 percent – and the rest is history!

How did you feel discussing *Iron Man* in that first San Diego Comic-Con?
I knew by the time they had that first teaser done that something would have to go very wrong for it not to connect with audiences. At Comic-Con my wife, Susan, watched me see it happen. And she said it was like all that confidence and bravado was very real because we were now in our own slipstream of feeling like we were doing something a little bit special and different. But the full circle of seeing that audiences were reacting to it the way we had hoped they would was a confirmation. I think it's hugely important to the human condition to feel that you get those kinds of validations.

You started something monumental.
I'd like to give credit where it's due. If you talk about

the business plan and how it unfolded for this, the major innovation was saying if we can do these three things, we can do this fourth thing. If we can do this fourth thing, we can do anything. And that to me was *Iron Man*, *Captain America*, *Thor*, *Avengers*, and then all of the amazing iterations that have occurred since. However, the first inning we pitched a shut out, so that helped!

Did you work out the chemistry before *Avengers* or was it just so well cast?
If you look at the amazing complimentary differences between the directors, Jon Favreau, Kenneth Branagh, and Joe Johnston, it's covering a lot of different bases.

And then we happen to smartly invite Joss Whedon to really try this Rubik's Cube of an execution. I remember the first *Avengers* just being a massive wrangling of all these different energies that had all been started from all of these different relationships and we synced them together.

Kevin Feige and Joss Whedon knew that there is a Civil War between Captain America and Iron Man, and we had to set that up somehow.

Where is Tony after *Civil War*?
He's on this eco-compound. It's the exact opposite of where Tony has physically been before.

Who is Thanos?
There have been rumblings of him in the ether as far

back as the first *Avengers* movie, and even in some ways before that. James Brolin is the sweetest guy you would ever want to hang out with. He's funny and all that, but I also feel like if he got it in his mind that he needs to evaporate half of every swirling sphere of life in order to live out what his own kind of karmic moral dilemma is, he would!

Thanos is essentially the least defeatable guy, the most cunning, and the most ambiguous about his motives. So that's something that has never occurred before. In *Iron Man 3* there was at least a false threat that wound up being an actor for hire. And that was our turnaround. Just by the way that Bruce Banner describes his interaction or understanding of Thanos, Tony knows that it's a different game now.

Thanos has got the best backstory you could ever ask for. As much as any of our heroes have had a conflict that is rooted in some sort of trauma that they survived, this is the one instance where he was one of us, and he went left instead of right. Ultron was our own mistake, and had a particular vendetta against his creator. This is someone who is literally an inter-dimensional and universal traveler. He's got a job to do, and he's got a reason he does it. And he does it very well. The audience can understand his motives.

Nobody in my generation has been raised without that crisis of overpopulation being kind of swept under the rug, because what are you going to do about it? So the idea that somebody's solution is to literally just cut it in half is almost biblical. It's about pruning the bush in the most heartless way you could imagine. He has the insight and the ability to be strong enough to do what we would consider inhuman acts.

Who have you had the most fun working alongside?
At first blanch, it's hard to know what to make of Benedict Cumberbatch. The more time I spent with him on and off

set, I've just become infatuated with this guy! He's so technically good and so untypically British. Doctor Strange was more obscure initially than Iron Man. I thought, *Man, that's going to be a real rough one to rise,* as it was his own origin story. The way he took the reins on that was super impressive and he executed the movie with a real sense of fun.

I always thought that Chris Evans had the toughest job launching Captain America. *How square is this guy going to be?* This is a man out of time. No one will buy it.

When we were considering who should be playing Spider-Man, I'd screentested with Tom Holland. I remember that feeling when I was about five years older than him, screentesting for *Chaplin*. It was just that first blush of opportunity and readiness. He's just such a capable guy and has become understandably confident based on how *Spider-Man: Homecoming* has performed. But also he knows how to fit in now, and he's got his own great ideas.

Chris Pratt is not unlike Cumberbatch. He's so approachable and sweet. And then he turns on that Iron Man-ish sort of wry, snappy humor in his own direction and reinvents it. It's funny when someone shows up with their own team because in this universe we like playing against the friction between just teammates. And now we are getting to expand that even more and start enjoying the friction between teams.

What have the last ten years of Marvel Studios movies meant to you?
It has literally been the adventure of a lifetime. I'm super grateful. I get a little misty thinking of hanging up my jersey, but there's nothing less classy than someone who sticks around after the party. So everything's in good stead.

What can fans expect from *Avengers: Infinity War*?
I guarantee you, *Infinity War* is nuts. Ⓐ

01 The Stark-designed Hulkbuster armor is called into service in Wakanda!

02 Tony Stark forms a fractious alliance with Doctor Strange in New York as Bruce Banner and Wong look on

02

CHRIS EVANS

CAPTAIN AMERICA

CHRIS EVANS
CAPTAIN AMERICA

Chris Evans returns as Captain America, a man out of time and out of sync with the country he has sworn to defend!

How have the events of *Civil War* changed Steve Rogers?
In *Captain America*, it's pretty clear that Nazis are bad. We can all agree with that. In *The Winter Soldier*, SHIELD is being run by Hydra. In *The Avengers*, aliens are no good, and we want to fight them. It's always pretty cut and dried for Steve to know which side of the coin to fall on. In *Civil War*, the conflict is a little more akin to the day-to-day struggle that we all go through where there's no right and there's no wrong. There's a point of view and I think it's hard for him to understand what the right thing to do is and what his role is.

Cap's always been a company man. He takes orders and he's a military guy, so if the government feels that something is for the best, who is Steve to question it? Tony, by the same regard, is someone who dances to the beat of his own drum and does what he wants to do how he wants to do it, so you wouldn't expect him to want to sign any type of accords or documents.

Steve's going through a lack of trust for other people. He's in multiple situations in his life. He's seen governments fail, so I think he feels that he is the most trustworthy. Tony's going through a bit of a guilty conscience. He's feeling a little bit more of a need to owe someone an allegiance as opposed to doing things the way he always wants to.

Steve and Tony's conflict is not enemy vs. hero. They're friends – almost like family. Sometimes the most dramatic conflict is when it's people that actually have a history and care about each other.

Is it fun to bring all these other characters into the film?
It's great. Marvel's so good at weaving this giant blanket together, so any time we bridge between worlds and universes and films it's exciting. You get to blend these universes and it's a real treat.

Is it hard for him because he's been so close with Black Widow?
That's what made the events of *Civil War* so tragic because we've all been close with everyone. Black Widow and Cap have had some beautiful moments and they really bonded in a lot of ways. Tony and Cap is the most heartbreaking friendship to see broken up. They're very different but that's what makes them such a unique pairing.

What's Steve's relationship like with Bucky?
Bucky is Steve's best friend – his oldest friend in the world. I don't think Steve is the kind of guy who grew up as Mr. Popular, so Bucky was the guy who has always been there. He's always had his back and Steve's a loyal guy. I'm sure there's a certain sense of guilt based on what happened to Bucky, but all their tragedies just brought them closer.

What do you enjoy about working with the Russo Brothers?
I love the Russos. They're great. They're just very easy-going guys. They're not pretentious. They have this encyclopedic knowledge of film. They're wonderful at being able to reference other films to bring people to a common ground. I always feel like cinema is such ▶

44 | *AVENGERS: INFINITY WAR*

01

> "Captain America is just a good man. Any time you get to go to set and process scenes through the eyes of someone who sees life a certain way, you can't help but take some of that home."

01 Down but not out, Steve Rogers is ready to defend the world

02 Loyal friends Black Widow and Falcon are never far from Steve's side

03 Even without his famous shield, Captain America is armed and dangerous

a subjective, creative outlet. Trying to get everyone to make the same movie, it's easy to get lost in a semantic fog. The Russos have a really good way of bringing everyone to the same page and making sure we're all making the same movie. They're technicians, which I really like. They're quick and they're precise. They know what they want and we just have a pretty good line of communication open between us.

What do you enjoy most about playing this character?
He's just a good man. Any time you get to go to set and try and live in a headspace for a certain amount of time and process scenes through the eyes of someone who

sees life a certain way, you can't help but take some of that home. Why not take home a little bit of Steve?

What's it like to wear the Captain America suit?
It's hot in that suit. You get a stuntman to do it if you can! It's tough. Some days there's no choice, you just have to be out there and you just try and focus on how cool it's going to look in the end. You maintain some perspective.

How's it been, working with Chadwick Boseman?
He's been great. He's a phenomenal actor but that's what Marvel does. They go out and they find the best.

02

03

What did you think of his Black Panther suit?
It's amazing. Every time you see these new suits it's like, "Oh! That's another cool character!"

Is it fun for you to play the more grounded, human moments in the film?
Those moments are in all the films. You never go into the *Avengers* movies thinking, *I'm gonna play this like a comic book*. You do your job and the way the movie looks in the end and the way it's edited is not up to me, so you always go into it trying to play the grounded version and trying to play the real version.

Are you ever surprised by the final cut of the Marvel Cinematic Universe films?
The thing about these movies is so much is done in post-production. When you're making the movie you have no clue. You come back six months later and you're like, *Oh wow, that's what it's gonna look like!* Ⓐ

SCARLETT JOHANSSON
BLACK WIDOW

Making her debut in *Marvel Studios' Iron Man 2*, Natasha Romanoff's skill as a spy and assassin makes her one of the deadliest Avengers. Actress Scarlett Johansson returns to her most dynamic role as one of the team's founding members.

Where do we find your character at the start of Marvel Studios' *Avengers: Infinity War*?
It's hard to say because there is a two-year period between *Civil War* and the start of *Infinity War*. I think there's a lot to explore there. I kind of built a back story for my own character that really finds Natasha in a place where she is more determined than ever to be as strategic as possible.

To keep everything under control as much as she possibly can, she's gone rogue. She and Steve Rogers are trying to monitor and take care of as much as they possibly can without having the Avengers around them. So we find them in a harrowing place. They're operating on their own terms. I imagine that Natasha is a little bit hardened from what she's experienced and having to police herself in a way. It's an unstable mental place to be in....

Where are Steve and Natasha in their friendship now?
I think Steve and Natasha have a very fluid communication between them. They've obviously been on hundreds of missions together, experiencing life-or-death situations. They operate very much like teammates. It's a kind of unspoken communication that they have at this point.

What does it mean to see this franchise through to this point?
It's been really exciting to get to work with some of the actors from different franchises that I have admired. We are an extended family – and then, of course, there are new characters that are also being introduced to the family, and that part of it is wonderful.

Marvel has really championed hiring actors that are unexpected, dedicated, and fresh. There's a lot of fresh faces now in this upcoming film. And Marvel really advocates new talent. That part of it is so exciting. It's bittersweet for me just to look around and see the cast and crew that have really become very close friends – like a movie family. I'm really proud of the work that we've done.

How is it to see more female faces in the group?
I've been advocating for some more female energy in the cast and crew as a whole for the better part of a decade. It's really great to see a more diverse group and to see that the audiences are embracing and even asking for female super heroines.

Is it fun to work with actors new to the franchise?
I love working with actors. If I can help another actor feel more comfortable or help them discover new choices ▶

01 Natasha and her teammates ponder their next move

02 A founding member of the Avengers, Natasha Romanoff faces an unexpected battle against the might of Thanos

03 Black Widow takes up arms as the battle against an alien force intensifies!

"Natasha's just trying to make whatever sacrifice she can in order to save her friends."

or help them to get acclimated to what could feel like a cool kids club, I'll do it.

It's nice that there are people in your workplace that you trust, so you can spread your wings and fly, and feel in a safe environment. I love to shepherd other actors in that way, it's awesome.

What is Natasha's take on Thanos?
It's very hard for her to access the exact threat of Thanos. He's certainly a force like she's never seen or could possibly even comprehend. She's going to come at Thanos with whatever she has and a lot of that is with her brainpower. I think she's really just trying to give whatever she can to the fight and make whatever sacrifice she can in order to save her friends.

We talk about Thanos so much before we see him that he's like a faceless evil. When we finally see him, the Avengers face the highest stakes that they have ever faced.

What have these ten years of Marvel Studios' movies meant to you?
It's been an incredible opportunity for me to be able to continue to come back to a character that I love so much and be able to peel back the layers of a character that I think reflects myself and reflects my own growth and my own challenges. I really feel it's been an incredible gift as an actor to be able to have that experience. I don't think there's many other opportunities that you have like that in film, to be able to continuously come back to a character that's as complex as Natasha. And I really feel that I've had an incredible opportunity to play this iconic character that means so much to people. Ⓐ

MARK RUFFALO
THE HULK

In order to play the formidable Hulk, actor Mark Ruffalo has to suit up, but not quite in the way that you'd expect…

How did you feel about the gravity and scope of this project?
I really didn't know how it was going to be possible. There are so many different storylines and about 71 speaking characters from the entire Marvel Universe and beyond. I thought it would be impossible to write across two different movies and bring in all the other movies and have it all make sense! I was really surprised when I read how cohesive it is and how well it tracks, and how successfully all the different mythologies come together and play off of each other.

What makes the Marvel Studios brand so successful?
There's a built-in audience that taps into several generations of comic book fans. I think we're hardwired for mythology. We want to see gods and monsters working out the problems of humanity in stories. Marvel Studios is really able to transcend all kinds of cultural divides.

I think what's really making it exciting now is diversity, not just a diversity of the players but also the diversity of the filmmakers. Marvel Studios allows each filmmaker to bring their own culture, mood, style, and creative input. It still holds. The characters are still the same characters. They're moving in and out of these different worlds, but the worlds are so vastly different. Each movie stands alone on its own. It doesn't look or feel imposed on by the filmmaker. They know how to hire really creative filmmakers that tell really interesting stories that are completely unique unto themselves. I think that's really been one of the keys to Marvel's success.

It just doesn't get old. You don't ever feel like, "Oh, I know what that's gonna be." When you look at *Guardians of the Galaxy* compared to *Civil War*, for example – they're each completely their own and unique things.

What's beautiful about these movies, and this movie in particular, is that you're bringing all these different worlds together, colliding them into one story. And that's exciting.

Where do we find Bruce Banner?
Coming out of *Thor: Ragnarok*, Banner is no longer really linked to the Hulk through anger. It's always been that Banner was struggling with excitability because he was afraid to bring out the Hulk. So he always felt like he was sitting on his emotions. In *Thor: Ragnarok*, Banner has been subjugated to the Hulk. Banner is not always angry anymore. He has a little bit more range as a character – he could get angry, he could get excited, he could get upset. I feel like Banner's reborn! He's like a 13-year-old kid.

He's much more able to express himself. He's not afraid of his own emotions. He's not afraid of fear or anger. But at the same time he can't summon the Hulk in the same way. The Hulk is separating away from Banner. He's starting to be able to be other things other than just angry all the time, and he wants an existence. ▶

01

02

"Bruce has seen the amount of destruction that is coming."

I always imagined this struggle, and I didn't know if it was going to be in some ethereal space where Banner and Hulk actually battled it out for primacy.

How is it for you to play that range now?
I was freaked out because people get used to a brand, and then they want it that way. We're playing with fire a little bit, but as a performer, Robert Downey Jr. was like, *what are you doing, Ruffalo? Why are you doing that?* I think part of the problem that we've had with making Hulk movies is people don't want to watch a guy who doesn't want to turn into the Hulk, as that is exactly the thing audiences want him to do! That can get old.

How is Bruce's relationship with Tony Stark?
They'll always be bros! They pick up where they left off. Banner in this film is like Chicken Little. He has seen the amount of destruction that is coming. They've been through Ultron, they've been through Civil War, he knows what's next.

I think he gets frustrated with Tony in a way that he's never been before. He and Tony have this antagonistic quality between them.

What was it like shooting the Wakanda scenes?
It's crazy. We all really enjoy each other's company, but there's that awesomeness of seeing the Marvel universes all coalescing into this one moment. And then all the other actors look so cool in their costumes while I'm wearing a suit that looks like a Chinese checkerboard!

How is Banner feeling about Natasha in this movie?
It's that classic unrequited love that all of us have experienced at one point or another in our lives, and for

"It's epic and classical. I feel like these characters are mythological."

▶ I feel like Marvel has definitely been moving into that light and darkness, so I wasn't surprised. It's refreshing actually that they've been building toward this.

What has this Marvel experience meant to you?
Ultimately, it's the people you work with every day. You are one of them. There are differences in experiences too, like the *Black Panther* experience versus the *Civil War* experience, and then in addition this experience where we have everybody here! That's something, no pun intended, you do marvel in. It's a cool experiment to be a part of. Everybody is genuinely trying to help each other, respecting one another. We're making jokes in-between; we're laughing all the time. So I think you really appreciate the work.

What do the Russo Brothers bring that sets them apart?
I think they literally see the movie in their head as they shoot it. And they see it like a fanboy and at the same time they see it like someone who is not part of that culture, of that niche audience. They're a dynamic duo, so they can split off and handle different things to disseminate responsibility amongst each other and amongst the other coordinators. They have a lot of great assets in terms of working with all of us as actors.

Were there any actors you were particularly thrilled to work with?
The Chris's! I was already able to work with Chris Evans. I knew Chris Pratt but we had never worked together. We've talked quite a bit and I knew he was cool. But it was just great to be out there with him. Chris Hemsworth, of course, is really funny and really fun to be around. I could say everybody. I love Mark Ruffalo; he's amazing. Everybody has been amazing!

What do you think audiences will connect to with these films?
I think people will enjoy seeing how the worlds clash, seeing how this character connects with this one. It's almost like having a movie of cameos. That's what you do when you read comic books – you look forward to the meetings between super heroes. So it's a feast in terms of that.

It's that emotional catharsis of trying to get to something that seems unbeatable and going through the pain of it, the tragedy of it. It's epic and classical. I feel like these characters are mythological characters in a lot of ways. But you have to go through that sacrifice to live up to it. Ⓐ

DANAI GURIRA IS

OKOYE

Remaining firmly by T'Challa a.k.a. Black Panther's side, the leader of the Dora Milaje is once again prepared for battle.

Where do we find your character in *Avengers: Infinity War*?
The Avengers are coming and they need support and help to deal with a very major global threat – a universal threat. And, of course, what I know is that Wakandans are the best to partner with when such a threat is hitting the world.

What does your character think of the Avengers?
She tends to play the devil's advocate, in a sense, for her nation, especially because her king, the Black Panther, has such a good, noble heart. So Okoye does tend to play that other side sometimes. They've had Winter Soldier as their guest for a while and he seems fine; he hasn't caused any trouble. So she understands the alliances that have been formed with these individuals and why these guys keep coming to us for help.

She seems pragmatic, whereas T'Challa is emotional…
They have a great balance between head and heart in that regard. We have now made ourselves clear to the world that this is where you come for help, so this is now our mission. And that's the evolution of Okoye to embrace, to let go of the isolationism, and to embrace the collectivism, letting these guys in and putting everything we have behind this battle.

Was it an advantage doing the standalone *Black Panther* movie just before this one?
It definitely was, because there was a lot of input we could share and feel out together because we know the context of where we're coming from. So in the scene where you see the Wakandans on the battlefield, we knew exactly how we would express ourselves, what moves we use, what war cries we use as Wakandans. So we came in with a lot of context.

What were the battlefield scenes like to film?
It was incredible! It was really amazing to be a part of that. Being on the battlefield with so many cool characters makes it a very intense battle. And so to see how that was all working out and how it was being staged and placed, and the vastness of the battlefield, it was pretty incredible. This is the sort of battle that could end the universe, so it was cool that it was happening in Wakanda!

Was it satisfying having such a big role in this movie?
It felt significant. It felt like there was a lot of substance behind the Avengers coming to Wakanda. It's set up in such a way to have a great amount of edge and suspense because we've seen Wakanda as a powerful nation, but we've also seen it have to battle with itself. And so the idea of being a part of this major moment for the Avengers made a lot of sense to me. It felt like very significant storylines were merging in a really palpable way.

Is it fun to play a strong female?
Oh, absolutely. I think there is something very powerful about being able to play women who are able to handle things, who are also strategists, who do heroic things and can take care of themselves. So it's been a really cool dynamic to play with.

Were there any actors you were particularly excited to work with?
Yeah! I'm a fan of so many people, but I'm very much a fan of Mark Ruffalo. I've really admired so much of his work over so many years, so it's been really, really cool to work with him and to watch him work, because the different nuances of the character he plays is just really fun.

What have you enjoyed most about this experience?
You really feel like you're part of a family, which is very special, not just with the people you're working with in front of the camera or the directors, but also the crew. 🅐

LETITIA WRIGHT
SHURI

Technological genius, and sister to T'Challa, Shuri returns to aid the Avengers in their fight against Thanos.

What did you think of joining the *Avengers: Infinity War* cast?
It was an honor because all of these actors are so gifted. I was super excited to be able to share the screen with them for like five seconds! I thought I would be super nervous but everyone's so chilled, easy-going, and super hard working.

Was it nice to have one Marvel film under your belt before coming into this one?
Super helpful because I already went through the machine, in a way. So the big experience wasn't a surprise. It was just a normal day on set. I was accustomed to how we were doing it, which took all of my fears away coming to *Avengers*. It was like, okay, cool, that's just Thor, and there's Iron Man. So it was great to film *Black Panther* first, get that out of the way, put so much hard work and love into it, and then come into this and do the same thing.

What was your Marvel knowledge prior to this?
I didn't know a huge amount, I would go to the cinema with my friends and watch *Captain America* or any Marvel film and still find the entertainment. Now that I'm a part of it, it's a pretty amazing universe! Because it's such a big thing going on, all the dots connect and you can just snip into different worlds. You have Thor's world, you have Iron Man's world, and you have Spider-Man's world. And you have Black Panther and the Guardians – it's huge! Now that I'm a part of it I appreciate it a lot more.

What is your character's take on the Avengers?
I don't know a lot about them. I know T'Challa, the Black Panther, has a lot of contact with them. He's a part of the Avengers team, he's on their side. We don't really interact with people a lot, so now we've opened up our borders, and our help, to others. But the more Shuri interacts with the Avengers, the more she realizes that her brother and Wakanda are a part of something much bigger than themselves, so they can't hide their help and their resources and their technology anymore.

Do you ever have a moment looking around you on set at all the actors?
A little bit, yeah. There are moments when I'm like, "Dang, that's Don Cheadle! I just played dominoes with Don Cheadle!" It's really, really cool. But then again, I'm so grateful because you realize that these amazing, talented superstars are really good people. They tell jokes on set, and they're just as hard working as well. But you do have those pinch-me moments where it's like, "Oh, man, this is actually happening!"

What makes Chadwick great as T'Challa?
I could say a lot of amazing things about Chadwick. There's a subtlety and an inner strength about T'Challa – he's not an introvert or an extrovert. It's a balance. The way he observes things, he takes things in so subtly, so beautifully. And the way he communicates with people and interacts with people, he's very caring, very loving, but also he has an inner strength that a king really needs. There's a love for his people and a love for what he does – I see that a lot in Chadwick.

He's not a man of many words, but you know he's thinking and he's engaging and he's sussing things out. He just has a good heart. But also he loves people, and he wants to do right by people, and as a king that's your first thing. You want to protect your nation.

What do you hope that audiences will enjoy about *Avengers: Infinity War*?
I hope that they can go on this journey with all of us wherever we take them in this story. When you get into that cinema, when you get your popcorn, when the lights go down, just enter into this universe with us and come on the ride with us to save everything from Thanos. I just hope everyone comes on the journey with us and that they love it. This is a pivotal moment in the Marvel Universe.

PAUL BETTANY
VISION

Created by the combined abilities of Ultron, Dr. Helen Cho, Tony Stark and Bruce Banner, Vision was brought to life by lightning from Thor's hammer. Paul Bettany returns as the android Avenger with a soul.

When you started working with Marvel Studios, could you have imagined what would happen?

Not at all. I kept the secret for about three years that I would be Vision. Jon Favreau just rang me up. We had acted in a film together called *Wimbledon*. He said, "I'm making this movie called *Iron Man*, and I'm looking for someone to play a totally characterless computer voice, and I just thought of you!" I said, "Thanks, Jon, that's great." And the rest is history.

It was a lot of fun. I'd go in at the end after the whole film had been shot. Everybody really liked me because whatever they hadn't managed to solve on camera, with CG or with reshoots, JARVIS could say something to fix the problem!

It took about 45 minutes, and then I went home. It was the greatest job ever! But then they decided to punish me by turning me into Vision! I think maybe it was Robert Downey Jr. who decided that I'd had it easy for too long!

What's it like wearing Vision's costume?

It is a hard costume to wear. I sit down on set and meditate. I think of the long line of actors that would love to be in my position. From that first day, getting in the costume and having the makeup put on was fine, but it all takes a long time. The costume is very claustrophobic, and it can get really hot. There is literally only a tiny amount of my skin left showing and even

that's covered in makeup. You can begin to freak out! For a couple of days it's fine, but by the third day I had to really focus on staying calm, which I think was probably quite helpful for playing the character!

What do you love about acting in this world?

Well, there's so much to like! I've enjoyed the character. I really love Vision. I'll never play somebody who is born on the screen, and who's both omnipotent and also naïve, again. That was really fun. And then seeing him learn what it is to try to become human has been really fun and interesting.

The really big questions for Vision are: *Why are we here? Why am I here and what is my ultimate purpose?* Seeing him try to figure that out has been interesting.

I've enjoyed the camaraderie with the actors and crew and production. I think there are a lot of things that differentiate this from other franchises. Just one of them is we've all got each other's back. We really like each other and we really love these stories and these characters. We've all known each other for a long time now. I've been doing this for ten years. My daughter was born in this period. Scarlett [Johansson] has become a mother. We've all had major life events happening whilst spending a lot of our years together. There's so much to look back on and in my old age I'm beginning to feel slightly sentimental about it as I hurtle toward my dotage! ▶

01

01 Can the romance between Vision and Wanda survive the events that threaten to engulf them?

02 Wanda and Vision unite on the streets of Edinburgh

▶ **The cast are all invested in their characters.**
Absolutely, and we often come across really hard scenes to accomplish because there's a lot of plot in these films. It's hard stuff to sell as an actor. I remember looking at Mark Ruffalo, Scarlett, and Don Cheadle. They are just so good.

It's hard stuff to do when we're talking about Thanos coming, and he's bringing an army that's going to destroy the universe. I was looking at them just full of admiration for how well they were doing it. We really care about each other and have been going through a life together.

How fun is it to have an onscreen relationship now?
It's been my favorite experience so far because it has got more complex. Vision's relationship with Wanda mirrors his investigation into what it is to be human. And it was a huge relief to not have to wear the Vision makeup for a couple of days! It was fun to be in disguise and that disguise be my face! Lizzie [Elizabeth Olsen] and I work well together. Everybody knows each other so well, so we don't have to be gentle. Everybody makes jokes about each other. If somebody messes up you make an incredibly vicious joke, and nobody takes it badly because we all know each other.

Where do we find Vision in this film?
We find Vision and Scarlet Witch incognito, meeting up in Edinburgh. It's a surreptitious meeting because, of

"I walked onto the set to film a camera test to see if the costume and makeup was going to work. Kevin Feige was there, and he cried when he saw me as Vision!"

course, when we last saw them in *Civil War* they were on opposing sides. And then everybody's drawn back together by a larger threat, and hostilities and grievances are absolutely put aside for the greater good.

How is Vision feeling about Thanos?
I think that the Vision is feeling very clear about what should be done with his stone, but his friends really don't want that to happen. They're intent on trying to save him.

How exciting is it to see the scenes with so many actors?
I'm often the first to arrive on set in the morning because my makeup takes so long. We were shooting the scenes in Wakanda in the middle of nowhere. As we drove toward the unit base, I thought, *Why are we in a town?* As I got closer, it was like the classic scene from *Star Wars* when they approach the Death Star: "That's no moon." It was not a town, it was the unit base. It was so enormous! I've never worked on a film where you were so aware of its size and potential. It felt like everybody was working on *Avengers: Infinity War*.

Are there any actors you're excited to work with that you haven't worked with before?
I'm a huge fan of Chadwick Boseman. I had met him really briefly when we were promoting *Civil War*. It was really lovely to sit down with him. He's just a really lovely chap.

How have these films stayed in the zeitgeist?
The people making the movies are fans. Everybody wants to make lots of money and be wildly successful, but I think the fans can sense that there's real love there. Right from when I became Vision, I walked onto the set to shoot a camera test to see if the costume and makeup was going to work. Kevin Feige was there, and he cried when he saw me as Vision!

There's a real sense of care for these characters and these stories. You can feel it every day on set, and you can feel it when you see the movies. If they bend the rules slightly within the universe they feel safe in, their fans feel safe in their hands and know that they have the best interests of those characters at heart. Ⓐ

02

ELIZABETH OLSEN
SCARLET WITCH

In *Marvel Studios' Avengers: Age of Ultron*, Wanda Maximoff –
the psionically powered Scarlet Witch – found herself on the wrong side
of the Avengers, before joining Captain America's team in *Civil War*. Now,
as the actress who plays Wanda, Elizabeth Olsen, explains, she and the
Avengers face their greatest test yet…

How has it been for you, getting to portray the same character across multiple Marvel Studios movies?
As the films have progressed with *Captain America: Civil War* and now *Avengers: Infinity War*, it's so nice to get to continue to have cool character arcs. I love the fact that Paul [Bettany, Vision] and I get to try and figure out this human experience, because with every movie he becomes more human and less like a robot. It's a very sweet thing to be on the other side of.

What was it like shooting those huge battle scenes in such a beautiful and historic city as Edinburgh?
It was really amazing to be in Scotland. I liked being on night shoots; it was kind of wacky, but I really enjoyed that. We got to see parts of Scotland lit up by our amazing Director of Photography. It was just gorgeous. It was a playground for us, bouncing off of these buildings, flying from one building to another. And blowing up the streets – it was really crazy getting to do huge special effects in such a tourist-driven area. There was real fire! It's really fun.

What do we learn from that Edinburgh sequence, and where does it lead you and the other Avengers?
With Thanos, we discover that he is interested in collecting all the Infinity Stones, one of which is in Vision's head. So our goal is to try and figure out how to remove it and destroy it. What does that mean for Vision? What does it mean if we take the stone out? If we destroy the stone, will it destroy him? There are a lot of questions and we have to try and figure it out.

What was it like coming face to face with Thanos?
The scenes I got to do with Josh [Brolin] were super emotional. He has such a penetrating voice, but he's in a polka-dotted onesie, so it's kinda distracting! But the voice that he's created and the detachment, this self-fulfilling narcissist, is really strong and defensive.

I also love working with Josh because he and I have worked with each other in the past. It was really fun to get to do something like this again. It's nice to have his energy around, and I think the scene that we filmed together was really powerful. It made me cry when I read the script, so I hope it impacts people.

Would you say there's a strong emotional component to this film?
I think that's always Marvel's great balance and goal – being able to have really cool action, but it doesn't mean anything unless you have substantial characters and storylines to connect with. And it is kind of the beginning of the end for a lot of these characters, who we've all been watching for a decade. ▶

"I've been flying a lot more [in this movie]. I became addicted to it!"

▶ **What do the Russo brothers bring to *Infinity War*?**
They approach everything with such a great sense of practicality. Like, what feeds the energy in a scene? How do we get from point A to point B? They want it to be more driven – energy driven, emotionally driven, physically driven. So they bring that perspective. Also, thank God there's two of them because it's crazy. Luckily we have two writers and two directors, and everyone's taking their turns moving around trying to help each other out.

How has it been playing such an interesting character?
She is a very strong, empowered person who might be intimidating to others. But I think that's the thing that's coolest about her, having so much emotional power and

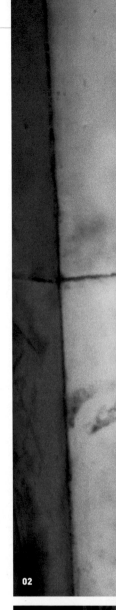

impact. That's part of her strength. I'm always trying to figure out ways to make her a little different to everyone else: 'How do I do that where it's more Scarlet Witch-y, instead of just reacting the way anyone would if they were a fighter?'

Wanda's powers seem to have evolved since we first encountered her...
With every movie I think we make her skillset a little bit more powerful. I get to do more things in this movie. I've been flying a lot more; Scotland is the first place where I was on the whole rigging thing, and that was about the craziest thing I'd ever felt. I became addicted to it! Also, the abilities I have, and what I can destroy and prevent – Wanda's been honing her powers and abilities.

How will these newly honed abilities manifest in this film?
You'll see her being able to do hand-to-hand combat as if she's been training as a fighter, but with her own abilities. So that's completely new.

Did you ever envision your character becoming such an integral part of the Avengers?
No, it's been a constant surprise, and if there's more to come after this, that will be another surprise. Every time it's been a whole new journey and more personal each time. I hope I get to keep doing these films, because it's been a lot of fun. My favorite thing is seeing people dressed up as Scarlet Witch. I have a doll – it's so weird – and it looks like my face. It's very strange!

What have been some favorite moments filming *Infinity War*?
Scotland was really special. That was a pretty cool experience. I got to know Paul a lot better as a person. And it was my first time really getting to know Mark Ruffalo. It's nice being able to call new people your friend. And I got to do a lot more stunt stuff.

There are always times when we all laugh too much during scenes and we can't focus. That's always my favorite time on set, when you can't get through a scene without laughing.

What do you think the audience will get from this film?
I think the reason why audiences are gonna connect is because they've invested the time. These characters have become so familiar that you already have stakes. You're already attached and committed.

I think we're gonna continue to surprise people. They're not gonna know what's hit them! I think the film is gonna be one of its kind. I don't think this has ever happened before in cinematic history, all these different franchises colliding. ✪

01 A pensive moment for Wanda Maximoff

02 The beginning of the end? Scarlet Witch's powers will play a big part in the fight against Thanos

03 Enjoying a romantic liaison with a more human-looking Vision

DON CHEADLE
WAR MACHINE

Colonel James Rupert Rhodes, known to his friends as Rhodey, is more than just Tony Stark's best friend. A highly decorated combat pilot, he is also a member of the Avengers. Don Cheadle first suited up in *Iron Man 2* as War Machine.

How has your War Machine suit changed?

War Machine has changed over the course of these films. At the beginning, we had actual metal pieces that I had to wear – a chest piece, leg piece, arms, the helmet, the whole thing. It was very difficult to move in, and I couldn't really touch my face. I couldn't drink or eat, and I had to be fed. It was like I was a turtle person – and that was challenging and hard to act in. You have no freedom, and you really have to figure out what positions you can be in.

Ultimately, you're trying to make the suit look like it's functional, so you're trying to move as elegantly as you can and as functionally as you can. It was really challenging! And then I think the next iteration of the suit was a little better, and there was more articulation. I could actually pick up a glass and get it to my lips, but it was still pretty cumbersome and didn't have a lot of mobility.

Did you have to use CGI?

They cut off the bottom half of the suit, so we just used motion capture. I had to wear those crazy colored pyjamas that are very embarrassing to wear and they take all of your dignity away!

With the newest War Machine suit, it's mostly the motion capture suit and the light-balls that they put on it. Before you shoot you have to do these yoga moves, and the cameras and computers capture all of that. Then they're able to map you when you're on the set. It's been a really fascinating progression over the course of the last nine years.

Did you have a sense of the Marvel Cinematic Universe when you were hired?

I knew that there were going to be *Avengers* films that War Machine could possibly appear in and potentially other movies. I was told that he might show up elsewhere because the Marvel Universe is vast.

But understanding the way that was really going to be laid out was something that still existed to a large degree in [Marvel Studios' President] Kevin Feige's head. I remember the first day trying to figure out how to be a super hero! *How should I stand? How should I hold myself?* You're asked often to deliver lines that are difficult – I think Chris Evans has the hardest job in that regard – but you're also trying to be faithful to these comic books and also to create a bridge for those who aren't comic book geeks and those who don't really understand the lore and the mythology. They just want to see an exciting, interesting movie.

What's happened since the events of *Civil War*?

The last time we saw Rhodey he was not in a great place. He was trying to come to grips with his service as a soldier and what he's supposed to do as a best friend and an Avenger. He's been badly injured and has paid a price, so it was nice to have a dramatic moment to underpin all of the action. And now we see him in *Avengers: Infinity War*, and through the benefit of Stark tech, he's been able to become functional again. He's back as an Avenger, and he's back on the team, but he's not forgotten what has happened.

What is the threat in *Infinity War*?

We saw the hole open in the universe a couple of movies ago, and Thanos is here to eliminate half of the population. The team takes a huge hit and we are left trying to figure out what to do. We're fighting the baddest of the bad this time, and it strains the relationships within the team. But the entire Marvel Universe comes together to fight against this ultimate evil.

I think this is the biggest film ever. The scope of what Marvel are attempting to do and how they're attempting to do it is huge. The technology that's around us on set every day and the things that we are witnessing and are a part of is fascinating. Just being in this world is awesome!

Why were the Russo Brothers right for this?

It's good to have two people who can be in the hunker and toss ideas back and forth and challenge each other and take this material, which is dense and vast, and disseminate this information to us. We're shooting out of order. It's a lot to wrap your head around, and they are somehow able to be the repository of all of this and keep us in the frame. If you look at the success of the other films, and you look at the cohesion of the other films, they clearly are the right people to do it.

Do you have a message for Marvel fans?

We're always appreciative of the support for these films. When we go to any of the Comic-Cons, we really get to feel the impact that these films have with the fans. And the fans really do connect to the films, and the films really are important and special to them. I think we all realize that we're doing something that's not just about showing up and punching the clock. We're really giving people something that they desire.

Rhodey's character has become more and more prominent, and he's finding his place in this group and getting to be more who he is. So it's great to have the opportunity to keep expanding. 🅐

> "We're fighting the baddest of the bad this time, and it strains the relationships within the team."

01

02

03

01 Is War Machine's arsenal enough to hold the forces of Thanos at bay?

02 Rhodey takes pause amidst the war

03 As seen in *Iron Man 3*, Rhodey is adept no matter what suit he wears

GWYNETH PALTROW
PEPPER POTTS

She's been there since the very first installment of the Marvel Cinematic Universe, but had no idea she was actually making history. Gwyneth Paltrow reflects on a decade of Pepper Potts.

It's been a ten-year journey for Pepper Potts from *Iron Man* right up to *Marvel Studios' Avengers: Infinity War*. How did you create your character's chemistry in the original movie?

I first met [*Iron Man* director] Jon Favreau doing a tiny independent Alan Rudolph movie in Montreal [*Mrs Parker and the Vicious Circle*] and we became friends. I had known Robert Downey Jr. separately from a very funny story that took place in the Toronto Film Festival – but we'll leave that story out…! So I always had a real fondness for him as well. And then one day they called me and they said "we really, really need you to do this part." I was semi-retired at the time. I'm still sort of semi-retired. They keep pulling me back into this Marvel Universe thing. But I got excited about the idea of going back to California and it just ended up being incredibly special. We laughed, we cried, and we got very, very close on that movie.

Was the spark between you and the others immediate?

I think Robert and I definitely work very well together – we have the same sense of humor. And then Jon was there elevating everything and making everything funnier and more intelligent and quicker. But I don't think you can construct that chemistry, it's something that is either there or it's not. And the funny thing is that in real life Robert and I have zero sexual chemistry. None whatsoever. But on screen somehow it translates. It's funny!

Whereabouts are Pepper and Tony in terms of their relationship now?

Pepper and Tony have had a really long journey together. She obviously starts as his dutiful assistant, and then the relationship evolves, and now this decade later they're married, and they have a child. Their relationship has evolved in all of the ways that great romances evolve.

Did you find the character of Pepper when you were filming on set or was she there on the page when you got the script?

In *Iron Man*, Pepper on the page wasn't that well developed. Jon knew that going in, and he was like "don't even really read it. You can bring a lot to it." Pepper is sweet and complex and smart, and she has an incredible love and devotion for this man, Tony Stark, and you see it progress throughout the course of all the movies. At the heart, there's an incredible love between them.

Would you agree that Pepper makes Tony more human?

I think a lot of it has to do with Jon's vision of casting actors who are maybe not necessarily associated with this genre before, and saying, "let's find great actors and put them in these genre movies and see what that might be like. Let's see what would happen if you were able to create that polarity." So you have the spectacle, and then I think the reason why you have those tender, human moments is because of the quality of the actors.

When you first started filming *Iron Man*, could you ever have imagined that it would build into what became the Marvel Cinematic Universe?

I could never have imagined it. We were having a great time. We thought we were making something cool that was sort of an independent movie fused with a big budget thing. But I certainly had no idea.

Have you had a chance to reflect on where these last 10 years have taken you, and that this chapter is coming to a close?

We've stolen moments to talk about the whole journey of these movies and how it started. There've been a lot of highs, and there have been a lot of lows and a lot of life lived, and I think all three of us recognize that we started something that was important. And it has gone on to really thrill and entertain and capture the imaginations of the audience. Jon gets very emotional, especially with everything coming to a close. We had a couple of tears over it. We're both probably more sentimental than Robert is in that way. Ⓐ

TOM HOLLAND
SPIDER-MAN

The youngest and most inexperienced Avenger, Peter Parker a.k.a. Spider-Man, is swinging back into action, once again played by Tom Holland.

Have you gotten used to being Spider-Man yet? I've changed a lot since becoming Spider-Man. Since filming in Atlanta and Avengers I haven't touched the floor once. I'm carried everywhere I go!

How much were you told about Peter Parker's storyline?
I just know that I'm Spider-Man. It's fun to take Spider-Man to space. You know, the space set we were working on might be the world's most dangerous set! So many people have fallen over on the set!

What's it like being an Avenger?
I remember actually going to see the first *Avengers* film with one of my best mates from home, and I'd never have dreamed that I'd ever be in one of these movies, let alone playing Spider-Man in one of these movies. So it's a dream come true for me to be here today. I've grown up watching all of the Marvel Studios movies and I'm a big fan, so being here today is amazing. I had two hours sleep last night, but I feel like I'm on top of the world because this is just mindblowing!

Your Spider-Man costume is very cool. Do you envy any of the other heroes' outfits?
I like Star-Lord's jacket. We were talking about how fashionable it is and how jealous of it I am. And look what I'm wearing! Ⓐ

SEBASTIAN STAN
THE WINTER SOLDIER

Friend turned foe, and maybe back to friend again, Bucky Barnes is called back into action after recuperating in Wakanda. Sebastian Stan returns as one of the most conflicted characters in the Marvel Cinematic Universe.

What was your reaction to the epic scope of the Marvel Studios films?

I didn't read a script, so there was no way for me to really know what my part in it was. But I was very humbled and excited to be included. It was interesting to see where they were going to take my character or what ideas they had with him at that point.

It's an understatement to say that we all have a pretty good time shooting these films. There's nothing to compare in terms of the scale of this film or the amount of people that I would see during the shoot. There were a lot of moments where I was really excited about it.

It's a lot of fun because I get to spend some time with the likes of Chris Pratt and all those guys. But from a character standpoint it's difficult because Bucky would freak out if he found himself conversing with a talking raccoon!

How does your character fit into Marvel Studios' *Avengers: Infinity War*?

My character is quite serious, but there's an element of comedy and a tone that comes in from the *Guardians of the Galaxy* and *Thor* characters. I had to adjust to that. In a way, I actually discovered more about Bucky because there were different places to take him in this film. He can be a little more on the lighter side, for example. There are more comedic moments and different nuances that weren't explored before.

He's resolved certain things in order to be called back in for battle. We get to see him at a more peaceful, calmer sort of place in Wakanda. He's in a more healthy environment where he can have another chance at learning about himself but then the call comes from Steve Rogers, and it brings him right back to where he was.

What was it like having the Winter Soldier become involved with the epic battle in Wakanda?

There were a lot of *Braveheart*-esque moments in the Wakanda scenes that I was involved with. I had goosebumps when I saw the scope of that battle.

The Russo Brothers were inspired by a large battle sequence that was staged in an episode of *Game of Thrones*. We took that battle and magnified it by about four times.

What is Bucky's relationship with Steve Rogers like now?

Regardless of what happens with the two of them, at this point in time there's a mutual understanding between them about a code of ethics and brotherhood.

It's like when you have two really good friends that don't see each other for a really long time. When you see them, you pick right up where you left off. It's very much in that same sense. Bucky just wants to be helpful. He's happy to get another shot and find a more redeeming side to his story, given what he was responsible for in *Civil War*. Ⓐ

THE GUARDIANS

ZOE SALDANA
GAMORA

SEAN GUNN (MOTION CAPTURE ARTIST)
ROCKET

DAVE BAUTISTA
DRAX

POM KLEMENTIEFF
MANTIS

KAREN GILLAN
NEBULA

CHRIS PRATT
STAR-LORD

OF THE GALAXY

01

Fresh from adventures in outer space, two worlds collide as the loveable rogues known as the Guardians of the Galaxy join the Avengers for a colossal showdown with mutual enemy Thanos.

Why have audiences connected so much to the Guardians?

Dave Bautista: Oddly enough, I think why people connect with them is because the characters are relatable. They're flawed characters. They're not so super hero-ish. James Gunn always referred to *Guardians of the Galaxy* more as a space epic and not a super hero film.

Chris Pratt: It's the type of super hero movie that you have to make now because audiences are way ahead of the game. We need flawed individuals as our heroes and people that we can get on board with and root for on a personal level, not just see them be exceptional.

Zoe Saldana: I was so confident that it would connect. All the messages felt relevant to me.

What will audiences love about the Guardians and Avengers worlds coming together?

CP: We're doing something the fans have wanted from day one. This is a giant spectacle. Essentially, it has cameos from every major character that's existed in the Marvel Cinematic Universe all coming together for this one epic two-part battle. And what the Guardians bring to it is it's irreverent, fun, slightly edgier, more cosmic, with great music and great chemistry, all between this ragtag squad of goons.

DB: I think that I'm one of those guys who, ever since the very beginning of even getting the job as Drax on *Guardians*, was really wishing that the worlds would collide and we'd somehow be involved in the crossover with the Avengers. That's really just me being a fan, I was hoping for it.

Pom Klementieff: In the Avengers movies you see a lot of action and they take themselves seriously. There are a lot of big things happening. But the Guardians are outcasts from the galaxy, we have some weirdness, and we're all so different and weird. I think we bring something light and more comedic.

01

"It's totally fun! After doing the two *Guardians* movies, I'm getting swept into this world and it's super cool!" -Sean Gunn

▶ **Sean Gunn:** It's totally fun! And it's kind of staggering in a way. I did not expect to be here. But after doing the two *Guardians* movies, all of a sudden I'm getting swept up into this world now, and it's super cool.

What is going on with these characters?
ZS: I think Peter Quill likes Gamora more than she likes him, for sure. But it's not because he's not the one for her, according to Gamora. I just don't think she's thought that much about love for herself. The last thing she feels that she deserves is love. He's that stupid brother that says everything wrong to her.

SG: Rocket has an interesting path forward in these movies because he changed so much in the second *Guardians* film. He was so surly and didn't give a crap about anybody, and then he learns to love a little bit.

DB: Mantis and Drax have a connection because there's an innocence to both characters. They're like two little kids, there's just a lot of stuff that Drax and Mantis can connect to, and there's a lot of stuff that both of them can't relate to. I think they'll always be bonded.

PK: They know each other a little bit more. They like each other, but there is nothing romantic or sexual about it, which I love. They just like to be next to each other and hang out and, you know, he feeds me nuts! I like their vibe, you know?

Karen Gillan: Nebula has always had a clear agenda throughout the *Guardians* movies, which is to seek revenge on her father Thanos because of the abuse that she has suffered. So to see that intertwine into the whole Avengers storyline is pretty satisfying, and now all of these other characters have the same agenda for slightly different reasons. It's exciting for me to hopefully see Nebula have her moment of revenge against her father.

Where is Nebula with Gamora?
KG: Nebula and Gamora had somewhat of a breakthrough where they started to empathize with each other a little bit and understand where each other was coming from and their points of view. When we pick it up in the *Avengers* movies they've definitely made progress, but they're still separated.

ZS: I think making peace with my sister is a part of the redemption. She's the only family member I'll ever know. There's no one else like me. Thanos made sure of that. So if Nebula's all I have, then she's worth the work and the pain.

What about Groot?
DB: It's great. I think it makes things a lot of fun because you get to see that annoying adolescent, the teenage Groot who doesn't want to be told what to do. And it's so funny because obviously Groot only says "I am Groot". But you pick up on everything that he's doing and it makes for a lot of fun.

01 The Guardians extend a warm welcome to Thor!

02 Groot, now in his somewhat surly teen years

03 Tiny tough guy Rocket (played by motion capture artist Sean Gunn and voiced by Bradley Cooper)

How do the Guardians react to Thor?

CP: My storyline with Thor is that I'm jealous of him, and I'm immediately competitive with him and failing miserably at trying to compete with him physically, emotionally, and with my voice. I'm seeing how enamored Gamora is with him and how the rest of the Guardians are with him, which hopefully is a mine for some comedy.

DB: Thor is passed out when we find him. We're all just in complete awe of him. You know, everybody's always, 'Oh, he's Thor, he's like a god. He's a god, man. He's so beautiful.' And we really, really played up on that. And, of course, Star Lord gets jealous immediately, which was so fun. And then we actually split because Thor has mistaken Rocket to be the smart one of the group and the captain as well, so there was a little friction there.

SG: Rocket takes a liking to him. And I think he feels sorry for him and even identifies with him a little bit. We see a tenderness that we hadn't seen too much in Rocket in the first couple *Guardians* movies.

KG: It's so much fun to see Nebula finally have the sense of family that I think she always craved. In the *Guardians* movies she is kind of invited into the family but is still hesitant because she's essentially an abuse victim. But now she actually finds herself as part of the Avengers, which is cool. And she develops a good relationship with Rocket and all of the other Avengers. These people are essentially her new family.

How are the Guardians linked to Thanos?

CP: When he has all the Infinity Stones he can take out half the universe with the snap of his fingers. And that's his desire. It's pretty evil.

DB: We are directly connected to Thanos through the death of Drax's family but also with his daughter being Gamora.

KG: We're all fighting against him, and it's an explosion of emotions for Nebula because of her past and what she experienced with him. The whole thing is a very emotional, bitter, and maybe weirdly cathartic experience for her.

PK: There is a lot of really beautiful and emotional stuff between Thanos and his daughters, scenes with Gamora, Zoe Saldana, and Josh Brolin that are really heart-breaking and really strong. It's really intense. I mean talk about daddy issues.

DB: We definitely have the most personal issue with Thanos. But also there's that wanting of revenge. So it really is a personal thing with us, we're not just protecting someone else.

What are the Infinity Stones and the Gauntlet?

CP: The stones have been the McGuffins for many of our movies. In this movie, there's the soul stone, there's the time stone, power. I think there's the reality stone, the mind stone.

KG: Thanos is after the Infinity Gauntlet. But first of all he has to retrieve all of the stones for the gauntlet because that will make him the most powerful being in the whole universe and essentially able to destroy everything. We can't let that happen. It would be very bad.

There are big pay-offs coming.

CP: People don't understand what they're walking into with this movie. The Marvel Cinematic Universe will never be the same following these movies.

KG: This is the biggest battle that the Avengers will ever face, ever. It's the ultimate war! And that just makes it terrifying – and kind of exciting.

What will audiences connect to in these films?

KG: They're going to be more than films. They're cinematic events! These are storylines that have been set up years and years ago. And if you've been following it then it's going to be one of the most satisfying experiences. The characters are amazing, the actors, the performances are great, and the visuals are the best out there. So I think people are just gonna be as awestruck as I am making them. Ⓐ

03

BENEDICT CUMBERBATCH
DOCTOR STRANGE

He may be a relative newcomer to the mighty world of Marvel on the cinema screen, but Benedict Cumberbatch feels now is definitely the time for Doctor Strange.

How did you feel joining the world of Marvel in 2016's *Doctor Strange*?
There was a bit of me, as an actor, that felt like I was coming late to the party. I'd seen the films. I'd had quite a few friends in the films as well. I didn't know what that experience was like as an actor. And obviously you're being hired because of what they want you to bring to the party. But you are still coming to the party halfway through, if not a third, two-thirds of the way. I'm thrilled. I'm really excited.

What's your advice to anyone coming on board the Marvel Cinematic Universe?
I think everyone wants something new, every Marvel experience they have to just forget what they're actually part of, because, sure enough, that thing envelops you as fast and as much as you could possibly know it will. So you have to play your line true to your character and be really strong in your intentions. Do your work. Don't worry about expectations and just please your director and your writer and Kevin [Feige, President of Marvel Studios], who's God. So that's pretty much it. And then we'll see how it fits into the rest of this huge old shebang...

Was there anyone you particularly looked forward to interacting with on *Avengers: Infinity War*?
All of them! Because I knew most of them. I'd bumped into them at various sort of events, like The Oscars. It's crazy. Kevin got very excited. He said "Oh, yeah, Doctor Strange is in *Infinity War* a lot." I was like, "Oh, is he?" It's utterly inspiring, the cast of this film. I mean really, really, really spoiling, really fantastic, very flattering as well and very securing. You think it's not just that I want to play this extraordinary character in a Marvel film, there are all kinds of other things that are attractive, such as the spread of the work, the challenges with the character, the action scenes and this extraordinary story.

What was your initial understanding of Doctor Strange?
It is strange in a way I suppose, no pun intended, that he's flown under the radar until now within the Marvel Cinematic Universe, because he is a very big presence in the original comics. It was maybe part of the master plan, because I think what we've seen happen within the Marvel Cinematic Universe is this ever-expanding coterie of super heroes. And from that everything kind of blossomed out into the more surreal, the more extraordinary, so that you can then have wormholes in New York. You can have otherworldly destruction happening in this world's space and time. I think now we're at the stage where this universe, even within our world, has got quite crowded.

And now things are really getting bigger...
And it's just about to explode into other dimensions! You've got Thanos, who's already sort of rumbled in the background a little bit. And I think Strange is a very natural bridge between what we know of New York or what we know of our sensual, sensory, perceivable reality, and something well beyond that.

What does is take for an actor to become a super hero?
You have to be fit. You have to have great core strength. You have to be able to hold yourself well. You have to move well. So you have to have fluidity as well as a training ritual to bulk up and get strong. I also did a lot of yoga, postural movement, and balancing work. That was a sort of shred every night: three hours of cardiovascular workout.

Did you have any accidents?
Yes! Quite a few. I've been hit in the face. I've been kicked in the stomach quite hard. I've been punched. I've fallen over. I've even tripped over the cape. That's happened a couple of times, which is not so super heroic, but it was very funny. 🅐

TOM HIDDLESTON
LOKI

Asgard's bad boy first smashed onto screens in 2011's *Thor*, and Loki has been creating havoc ever since. Tom Hiddleston gets into the mind – and horns – of the God of Mischief.

Did you know you were a part of something special when you were working on the first *Thor* film?
I had certainly thought we were making something unique. Certain fantasy films, they tended to be heavy on action and sort of light on drama and emotion. What was so brilliant about that first film is it felt like [Director] Kenneth Branagh really said, "I want to make a film that people find unbelievably entertaining, that's full of thrills and spills and action." Also a part of that experience was about adding dimension to the spectacle with feeling.

The thing fans really wanted to see was Loki's horns...
It was always like the missing piece of the puzzle of the character for me. In all my fittings, way back, I kept thinking, *When am I going to get the horns on?* Because it's almost like the last piece of the jigsaw to becoming the character. They just add an element of the devil to him. It feels enormously powerful.

Does this outfit really help your performance?
Hugely. Underneath I'm wearing a suit, it's like one big tight fitting thing which keeps my whole body locked together. It makes you stand tall and stand proud, and there's also something about the brow, it sort of makes you look out from underneath it which kind of gives you a bit of mischief. It's very heavy. I would lose literally 10 pounds per day in sweat, and would have to replace it with broccoli and steak, or ice cream. It was epic.

It's fair to say each outing for Loki feels that bit bigger...
We're not going small here! We're going as big as we can get and we're trying to create this huge story. It's enormously challenging in lots of ways because at the same time it isn't real. And you're surrounded by a crew of guys in jeans and t-shirts, and who are muttering about having a cappuccino and you have to – and this is every actor on every film ever – take your head away from the cappuccino and into the scene in question.

How has the relationship between Chris Hemsworth and yourself changed over the course of these films?
Chris and I, from the very first frames of *Thor*, we just really trusted each other, and when you trust the person you're acting with you can go so much deeper into the characters than you might otherwise do, you can reveal so much more and it's just so much more fun. One of the great pleasures of doing these films has been working with him, because we just sort of get it, and it's a really nice rare and unique relationship to have with an actor, where anything goes.

Do you think it's important to keep humor throughout the script too?
One of the greatest strengths of Marvel films, since the very first *Iron Man*, is that they have all had their tongue firmly in their cheek. We're inhabiting a very colorful world of larger than life characters who do wear capes and were originated with speech bubbles inside comic book frames. I think that's the great distinction of the Marvel films, and I really take my hat off to the studio.

What is it that you love about the fans of *Thor* and the way they've reacted to these films?
Well it's amazing. The fan responses are beyond any of my expectations, beyond any of our expectations, and what's so thrilling is that people seem to have taken these characters into their hearts and they really believe in the world. I love how the fans have really embraced the Marvel Cinematic Universe and follow and believe in it wholeheartedly. It's given us the confidence to go even deeper with it, and to say, "Oh wow, everyone really appreciates people having emotions in a blockbuster. Who knew?" ⏃

JOSH BROLIN
THANOS

Thanos is finally here! Actor Josh Brolin is ready to wield the Infinity Gauntlet as he takes on Earth's Mightiest Heroes...

What did you want to bring to the character of Thanos in this film?
Complexities. That's the thing, I'm doing two things at once; I'm getting used to a certain style of motion capture acting that I don't know. Everything was brand new, everything was newborn. So when I started to get into it, there was a natural vulnerability that I felt, and then started to take advantage of – this dichotomous nature of what a bad guy is. I always thought that if you could make five mothers in the audience want to fix this guy, then you've done your job. So I think we found some colors.

How much say did you get into your portrayal of Thanos?
They gave me a lot more leeway than I would've assumed. I thought that, given that this is a Marvel movie, given that this is storyboarded in such a major, major way, and so intricately and so specifically, that it would be like: this is what we've already figured out, so this is what you should do. But it wasn't like that at all. [The Russo brothers] would come in and they'd say, 'This is the general sketch of it, what would you like to do?'

When I first came in, I imagined Thanos as super formal, totally stiff, you know, sitting on a throne. As I got more comfortable, they kept cutting off whatever formality I had, like: 'Scratch your head, and just pick your nose and look at your booger if you want, and flick it.' And I'm like, really?

So then you start doing that. You think you've done the worst acting you've ever done in your life. And then they show you the visualization months later. And once they showed me, that was it. Then I got it. Then I understood the capabilities and the possibilities of what we were getting into, because it was so natural. The visualization was incredibly helpful.

Even so, it must have been a challenging experience.
From an acting point of view, it's been a real labyrinth to find my way through, and really challenging in the best way. This is stretching my imagination more than most things that I've done, because you have to fully imagine it.

Is it possible to sympathize – or at least empathize – with Thanos' motivations in this film?
You can fault him for his thinking, but it's the conviction of the thing. This guy sees this universal big picture. You start to follow his logic; if you look at a place that's overpopulated, you understand they are in the process of destroying themselves. So how can I fix that? Then it starts to make logical sense, even to me playing it. He's not a good guy, but it makes sense. What is he doing it for? Is he doing it to save the other half? And is that justifiable?

What is Thanos' aim in *Infinity War*?
He's going for all the Infinity Stones. He's going for all the power, under the auspices of trying to fix the universe. He's trying to balance the cosmos. And by doing that he's having to destroy a lot of things.

What he set out to do is extremely important to him. He was born a deformity, never accepted. What he's doing from his point of view is a very positive thing, but you can't take away from the fact that he is an anomaly, you know, a deformed anomaly. So he must be reacting to something.

In the movie, I think you go back and forth with understanding his conviction and what he's trying to do, and then what might be motivating it. It's personal, and then it's outside personal, then it becomes personal again, and outside personal... And I think that's what's been really fun about the character.

▶

> # "I've never felt so comfortable on a movie set. It's a family and everybody's idea is valid."

Tell us about the relationship between Thanos and Gamora.
She grows up into a very complex character. There's a lot of contention there and a lot of strife, but also a lot of love, because he did raise her. So she's struggling with this thing constantly. He treats her like his most precious, prized daughter, even though she's not his daughter – Nebula is.

What's been your favorite aspect of making these films?
It's gonna sound so lame, but every time I come back here it always feels like I'm coming home. I've never felt so comfortable on a movie set. I've never felt a crew so married to each other. It's truly familial here. It's a family, and everybody's idea is valid. It's a great crew, you know?

What makes working on a Marvel movie special?
It's the right collective. It's like… when you have theater collectives, and you're putting this thing together, and trying to find the color in everything, and the social significance, and the personal significance, and all this stuff – that's what this feels like. This feels like a theater troupe got together – and somebody gave them 500 million dollars by accident. Ⓐ

01 Thanos brandishes the Infinity Gauntlet

02 Josh Brolin performs his role as Thanos

03 The conqueror from Titan, victorious?

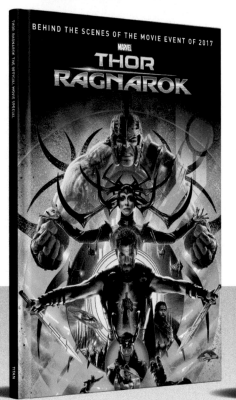

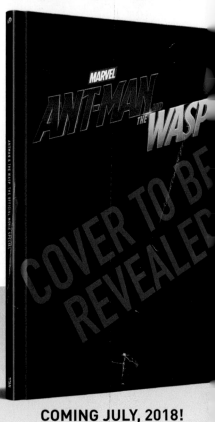

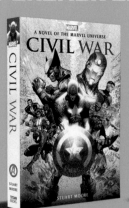